THE HEART-SHATTERING FACTS ABOUT THE TRAIL OF TEARS

US History Non Fiction 4th Grade

Children's American History

BABY PROFESSOR

EDUCATION KIDS

Speedy Publishing LLC

40 E. Main St. #1156

Newark, DE 19711

www.speedypublishing.com

Copyright 2017

Before Europeans made homes in what is now North America, the land was full of millions of Native Americans. They were part of hundreds of tribes, and had lived in harmony with the land for thousands of years. How did things change for the Native Americans? Read on and learn the sad story of the Trail of Tears.

NATIVE PEOPLE AND SETTLERS

As Europeans settled in the new world, they had a complex relationship with the people who lived in the land. In some areas, like Rhode Island under Roger Williams, Native Americans and settlers had a good and respectful relationship. To learn about the violent end to that period, read the Baby Professor book King Philip's War.

ROGER WILLIAMS STATUE

In the south of the United States in the 1830s, over one hundred thousand Native Americans still lived on what had been their traditional lands. Before 1850, almost all of them were gone, either dead or forced out of their lands and into the land of other tribes or onto country that was very poor and could not really support a lot of people

THE "CIVILIZED TRIBES"

European settlers often had a very negative attitude toward Native Americans. Some people feared they would be attacked and scalped, not knowing or remembering that it was the British Army that had taught their Indian allies to scalp their enemies and bring the scalps in as proof of how many people they had killed.

SCALPING SKILL

NATIVE AMERICANS SIMPLE LIFE

Other settlers disapproved of the Native American way of life. For the Europeans, the new world was open land to be developed and exploited, but the tribes tried to live in harmony with the Earth, doing as little harm as they could to get what they needed to survive. The settlers thought this was "uncivilized" and wasteful.

Some settlers, including President George Washington, felt that the solution to the "Indian problem" was to teach Native Americans how to live like white Europeans, holding jobs, working for money, and living in settled communities. They did not see that the Native American life had value.

PRESIDENT GEORGE WASHINGTON

SEMINOLE FAMILY

Some tribes in the American South tried to find a way to live and work in harmony with the new arrivals. People of the Chickasaw, Seminole, Cherokee, Creek, and Choctaw nations were even known to white Americans as the "five civilized tribes."

But at the furthest extreme, some white Americans held that Native Americans were not really human, that they were two-legged animals without souls or rights. These people believed that the only good Indian was a dead Indian.

INDIAN REMOVAL

For white Americans, the biggest problem was that Native American land was valuable. It was good growing land with excellent natural resources. White America wanted to exploit those resources to the fullest, and did not care what the Native Americans thought about the matter.

Settlers burned Native American villages and stole their animals. They took land that had been granted to Native Americans in treaties, and killed warriors who tried to stop them.

Some state governments passed laws limiting the rights of Native American tribes and taking some of their land. Even when the U.S. Supreme Court ruled that the states were wrong and that the tribes had treaty rights, the states ignored the rulings and kept the pressure up on the tribes.

President Andrew Jackson, in the 1830s, supported removing the tribes from the land white Americans wanted. When he was in the army, Jackson had fought merciless battles against tribes in Florida, pushing them off hundreds of thousands of acres of good land. As president, he signed the Indian Removal Act in 1830. This act gave the government the right to take away the tribes' traditional lands in exchange for land in the far west of the United States.

PRESIDENT ANDREW JACKSON

OKLAHOMA

This land, in what is now Oklahoma, not only would not support the life and culture of the tribes of the southern states; other tribes already considered it their land. The United States government was creating a situation where tribe would fight against tribe for much less in the way of land and resources than the Native Americans had had before.

The law said the government should work out fair plans with the tribes for the exchange of land. In practice, the government often ignored what the law said and pushed the Native Americans west, sometimes with violent attacks.

THE TRAIL OF TEARS

The Choctaw people were the first tribe to be evicted from their traditional land, in 1831. They were forced to walk to their new territory, some chained together to keep them from escaping. They had little food or supplies, and, once they got to Indian Territory, no help from the government.

CHOCTAW GROUP

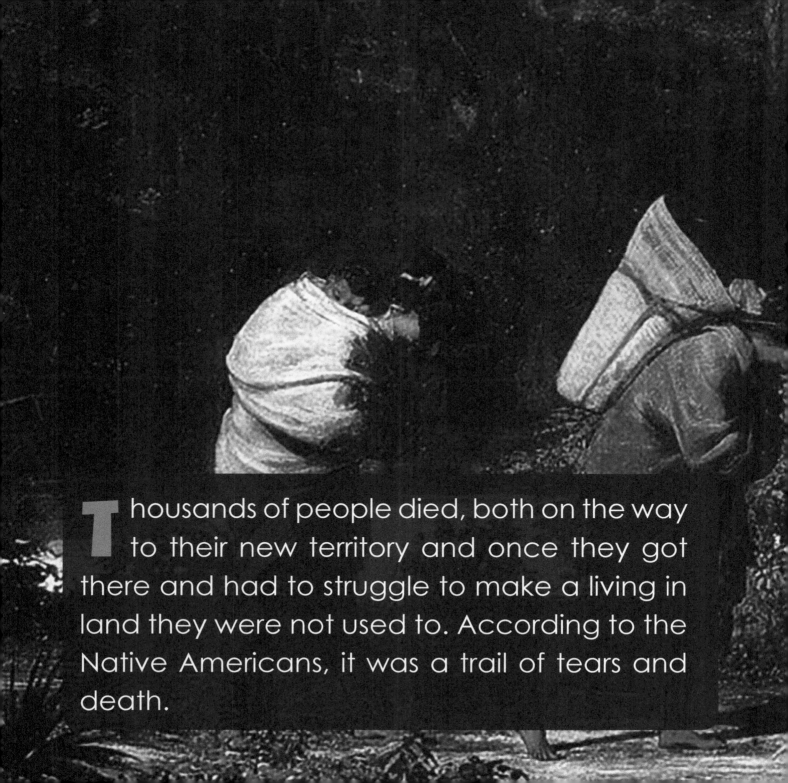

Thousands of people died, both on the way to their new territory and once they got there and had to struggle to make a living in land they were not used to. According to the Native Americans, it was a trail of tears and death.

In 1836 the federal government forced fifteen thousand members of the Creek tribe from their land. Over three thousand people died during their walk to Oklahoma.

some members of the Cherokee people signed an agreement giving their traditional lands to the federal government. Many in the tribe said the treaty was not valid, because the Native Americans who signed it did so without any authority. The United States government said the treaty was valid.

CREEK WAR TREATY

CHEROKEE PEOPLE

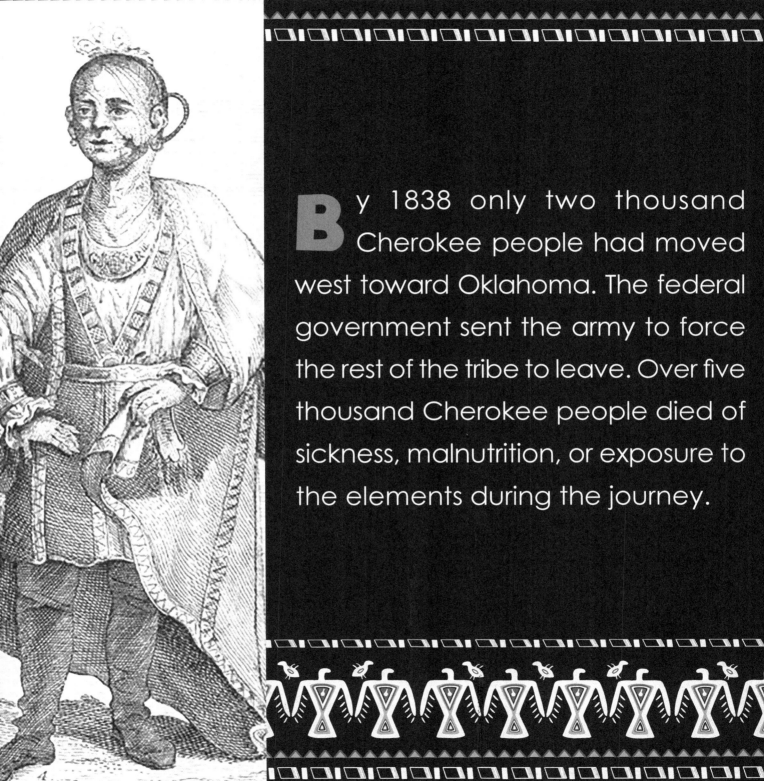

By 1838 only two thousand Cherokee people had moved west toward Oklahoma. The federal government sent the army to force the rest of the tribe to leave. Over five thousand Cherokee people died of sickness, malnutrition, or exposure to the elements during the journey.

More than thirty thousand Native Americans were forced off their traditional lands, across the Mississippi River, and into Indian Territory by 1840. Many thousands more had died from their cruel treatment at the hands of the federal and state governments.

MISSISSIPPI RIVER

Oklahoma and Indian Territories

OKLAHOMA AND INDIAN TERRITORIES

The tribes had been promised that Indian Territory would be land for Native Americans forever. But the United States continued to grow and expand, and continued to make the land of the Native Americans smaller and poorer.

In 1907, what had been Indian Territory became the State of Oklahoma, and the only territory Native Americans still had was reservation lands. Read about these lands in the Baby Professor book Are Indian Reservations Part of the US?

ARDMORE, INDIAN TERRITORY, 1891

DAVY CROCKETT

FACTS ABOUT THE TRAIL OF TEARS

Not every white American agreed with the government's plans, and not every Native American went along with it peacefully.

DAVY CROCKETT

Crockett was a famous explorer and frontiersman. He had been an army scout under Andrew Jackson during the Creek War in 1813-1814.

But when he was a member of the U.S. Congress, Crockett opposed Jackson's plans for removal of Native Americans from their lands. Crockett argued hard against the actions of the government, both under President Jackson and under President Van Buren, who followed him.

PRESIDENT MARTIN VAN BUREN

Crockett was so disgusted that he left the United States to live in the Mexican territory of Texas. He died fighting for Texan independence from Mexico in 1836.

ONE VOTE

The treaty with the Cherokees, which the Native Americans claimed was not valid, passed the U.S. Senate with a margin of one vote in 1836, and President Jackson signed it into law.

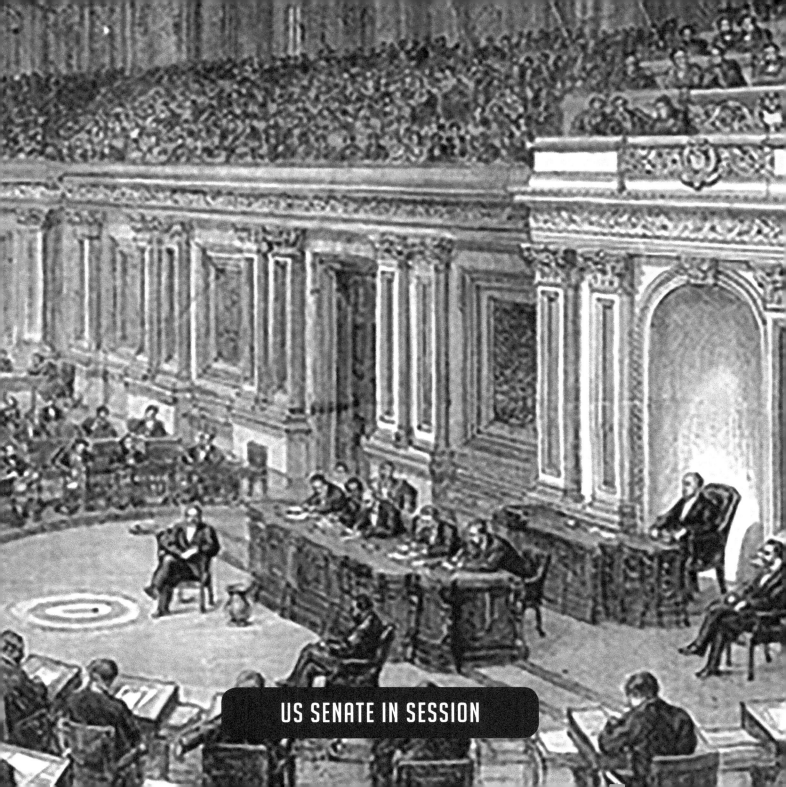

US SENATE IN SESSION

JOHN ROSS

MANY TRAILS OF TEARS

The Cherokees were forced out of their lands along many trails, and some were even transported for part of the way by boat. Cherokee Chief John Ross divided the tribe into thirteen groups, each of about one thousand people. Almost everyone had to walk, no matter how healthy or sick they were, or what group they were part of. The distance was almost a thousand miles.

A TWO-YEAR MARCH

The expulsion of the Cherokees started in 1836. The last groups arrived in Indian Territory in early 1839.

Unorganized Territory

Cherokee   Claremore
                      181

Creek +
Seminole   Fort G

Chickasaw   C

MEXICO
(from 1845 Texas)

Indian Removal

Cherokee	
Chickasaw	
Choctaw	
Creek	
Seminole	

Tribal territory

Reservation

Kilometers
0   50   100   150

0   50   100

Miles

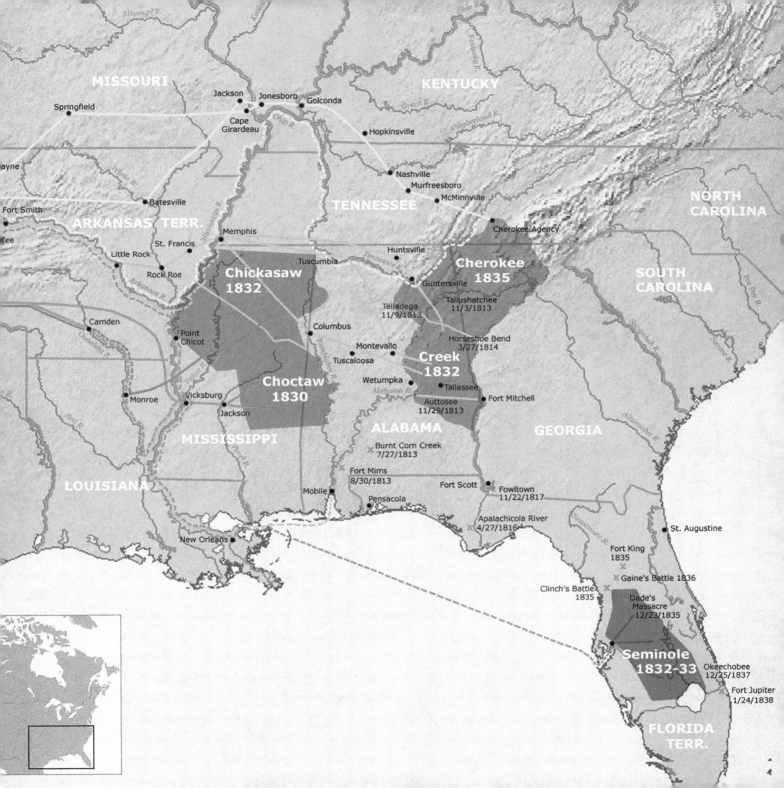

A REMNANT

Small groups of Cherokees managed to avoid expulsion and stayed in North Carolina. Some had been part of an agreement signed in 1819 that let them stay on their own land. Others walked back from Indian Territory in the years after 1840. The descendants of this group, over twelve thousand people, are known as the Eastern Band of Cherokee Indians.

AFTERMATH

Survival in Indian Territory was very difficult, especially as the people were short of supplies and had to learn their new land. The Cherokee tribe gradually built back up in the 1840s and 1850s under Chief Ross.

GROUP OF NATIVE AMERICANS

CIVIL WAR

When the Civil War broke out in 1861, the Cherokee people first tried to stay neutral. Then they allied with the southern Confederate states in hopes of getting their ancient lands back.

After a while, the tribe broke with the Confederacy and tried to be loyal to the United States.

Chief Ross died in 1866, just after the end of the war, having led the Cherokee Nation through terrible times for most of his forty years as chief.

APOLOGY

In 2009, the U.S. government passed a resolution apologizing to the Native American tribes for their treatment during the time of the Trail of Tears and after, and for all the times the federal government broke its solemn promises. However, the resolution did not include any measures to return to the tribes what had been taken from them.

THE PEOPLES OF NORTH AMERICA

Learn more about the complex cultures of the Native American people in Baby Professor books like Getting to Know the Great Native American Tribes and The World is Full of Spirits: Native American Religion, Mythology and Legends.

Visit

BABY PROFESSOR
EDUCATION KIDS

www.BabyProfessorBooks.com

to download Free Baby Professor eBooks and view
our catalog of new and exciting Children's Books

CPSIA information can be obtained
at www.ICGtesting.com
Printed in the USA
BVHW012157020120
568457BV00011B/166/P

9 781541 911826